Assessment of the Chief Executive REVISED EDITION

A Tool for Nonprofit Boards

By

Joshua Mintz and Jane Pierson

BOARDSOURCE
Building Effective Nonprofit Boards

CAVANAUGH
HAGAN &
PIERSON
Counsel to Organizational Leaders

Library of Congress Cataloging-in-Publication Data

Mintz, Joshua.

   Assessment of the chief executive : a tool for nonprofit boards / by Joshua Mintz and Jane Pierson.--
2nd ed.

      p. cm.

   Rev. ed. of: Assessment of the chief executive : a tool for governing boards and chief executives of
nonprofit organizations / by Jane Pierson and Joshua Mintz. 1995.

   ISBN 1-58686-089-5 (pbk.)

   1. Nonprofit organizations--Management. 2. Chief executive officers. I. Pierson, Jane. II. Pierson,
Jane. Assessment of the chief executive. III. Title.

HD62.6.M558 2005
658.4'07125--dc22

                                                            2005009777

Published by BoardSource
1828 L Street, NW, Suite 900
Washington, DC 20036

BOARDSOURCE
Building Effective Nonprofit Boards

BoardSource, formerly the National Center for Nonprofit Boards, is the premier resource for practical information, tools and best practices, training, and leadership development for board members of nonprofit organizations worldwide. Through our highly acclaimed programs and services, BoardSource enables organizations to fulfill their missions by helping build strong and effective nonprofit boards.

BoardSource provides assistance and resources to nonprofit leaders through workshops, training, and our extensive Web site, www.boardsource.org. A team of BoardSource governance consultants works directly with nonprofit leaders to design specialized solutions to meet organizations' needs and assists nongovernmental organizations around the world through partnerships and capacity building. As the world's largest, most comprehensive publisher of materials on nonprofit governance, BoardSource offers a wide selection of books, videotapes, CDs, and online tools. BoardSource also hosts the BoardSource Leadership Forum, bringing together governance experts, board members, and chief executives of nonprofit organizations from around the world.

Created out of the nonprofit sector's critical need for governance guidance and expertise, BoardSource is a 501(c)(3) nonprofit organization that has provided practical solutions to nonprofit organizations of all sizes in diverse communities. In 2001, BoardSource changed its name from the National Center for Nonprofit Boards to better reflect its mission. Today, BoardSource has approximately 8,000 members and has served more than 75,000 nonprofit leaders.

For more information, please visit our Web site, www.boardsource.org, e-mail us at mail@boardsource.org, or call us at 800-883-6262.

Have You Used These BoardSource Resources?

VIDEOS

Meeting the Challenge: An Orientation to Nonprofit Board Service
Speaking of Money: A Guide to Fundraising for Nonprofit Board Members

BOOKS

The Board Chair Handbook
Managing Conflicts of Interest: Practical Guidelines for Nonprofit Boards
Driving Strategic Planning: A Nonprofit Executive's Guide
The Board-Savvy CEO: How To Build a Strong, Positive Relationship with Your Board
Presenting: Board Orientation
Presenting: Nonprofit Financials
Meet Smarter: A Guide to Better Nonprofit Board Meetings
The Board Building Cycle: Nine Steps to Finding, Recruiting, and Engaging Nonprofit Board Members
The Policy Sampler: A Resource for Nonprofit Boards
To Go Forward, Retreat! The Board Retreat Handbook
Nonprofit Board Answer Book: Practical Guide for Board Members and Chief Executives
Nonprofit Board Answer Book II: Beyond the Basics
The Nonprofit Legal Landscape
Self-Assessment for Nonprofit Governing Boards
Dollars and Sense: The Nonprofit Board's Guide to Determining Chief Executive Compensation
Fearless Fundraising
The Nonprofit Board's Guide to Bylaws
Understanding Nonprofit Financial Statements
Transforming Board Structure: New Possibilities for Committees and Task Forces

THE GOVERNANCE SERIES

1. *Ten Basic Responsibilities of Nonprofit Boards*
2. *Financial Responsibilities of Nonprofit Boards*
3. *Structures and Practices of Nonprofit Boards*
4. *Fundraising Responsibilities of Nonprofit Boards*
5. *Legal Responsibilities of Nonprofit Boards*
6. *The Nonprofit Board's Role in Setting and Advancing the Mission*
7. *The Nonprofit Board's Role in Planning and Evaluation*
8. *How To Help Your Board Govern More and Manage Less*
9. *Leadership Roles in Nonprofit Governance*

For an up-to-date list of publications and information about current prices, membership, and other services, please call BoardSource at 800-883-6262 or visit our Web site at www.boardsource.org.

Contents

Introduction

The job of the chief executive can be a lonely one. With no peers and no direct supervisor, it can be difficult for the chief executive to obtain honest feedback essential to improving his or her performance. An assessment can provide leaders with answers to the questions: "What am I doing well?" and "What can I do better?" By conducting an assessment, the chief executive has the opportunity to receive the needed insight into his or her strengths, limitations, and overall performance. The consequences of failing to assess the chief executive can lead to mistrust, strained working relationships, ongoing poor performance, and even turnover.

In too many nonprofit organizations across the country, the board seldom takes the time to assess the chief executive's performance. Why is assessment so often neglected? Some boards feel that it requires too great a commitment of time and energy. Others are reluctant to open a can of worms when things seem to be going just fine. Often the board and the executive have mixed emotions about giving or receiving candid feedback. Chief executives may resist assessments when they think the board doesn't have the information to fairly conduct an assessment or fear that the board may take this as an opportunity for micromanagement. But most often, boards simply don't know where to begin.

WHY CONDUCT AN ASSESSMENT?

Assessing the chief executive is one of the board's primary governance responsibilities and is critical to the success of the chief executive and the organization as a whole. Therefore, there are a number of reasons why a board should perform this annual assessment. First, boards must clarify their expectations for the chief executive. A common refrain from many chief executives is, "If I had known they expected that, I would have focused on it!" If the board and chief executive together have not clarified the executive's priorities for the year, it is then up to the executive to create his or her own priorities, which may or may not be aligned with those of the board. This can lead to conflict. Establishing a set of priorities can help ensure that everyone shares common expectations for the chief executive's performance.

The assessment process also provides the board with the opportunity to say "Well done." While some boards may use the assessment to find fault or problems, most boards enter into the process with a positive outlook and a desire to strengthen the chief executive's performance and effectiveness. In fact, the outcome of the assessment can often result in a strong endorsement of the executive's performance. Most important, the chief executive's performance affects the performance of the entire organization — one of the board's chief concerns.

The timing of the process should be linked to the organization's annual calendar and planning cycle so that the board will be able to assess the entire year's performance and begin a discussion of annual performance goals for the year ahead. For this reason, most organizations conduct the assessment at the end of the year (calendar or fiscal). Regardless of the timing of the assessment process, it should be completed before any discussions of compensation are held.

WHO SHOULD PARTICIPATE?

Because it is a board responsibility, the primary group of respondents should be limited to board members and the chief executive. In some cases, depending on the size, complexity, and culture of the organization, it may be appropriate to obtain input from senior staff members who have a closer working relationship with the chief executive and may be able to provide important insight into his or her performance. If staff members are included, it is important to analyze the board and staff responses separately so that the unique perspectives of these groups can be distinguished.

External informants should not be included in the assessment process. Should the board want information on how the organization or chief executive is viewed externally, the organization should conduct an external review or organizational audit.

ABOUT THIS TOOL

The *Assessment of the Chief Executive: A Tool for Nonprofit Boards* is divided into four main sections: Annual Performance Goals; Core Competencies for Nonprofit Chief Executives; Personal Leadership Qualities; and Accomplishments and Challenges. The ratings reflect how well the chief executive's performance has met the board's expectations: failed to meet expectations, met expectations, or exceeded expectations. There is also an option to answer "Not Applicable" to questions that do not apply to the executive's job. The board and the chief executive are asked to complete the same assessment form, making it easier to evaluate and compare both sets of scores.

Section 1 allows the board to evaluate the chief executive's performance around specific, previously established annual goals. All assessment participants should refer to their particular organization's list of goals for the chief executive.

GOALS FOR THE ASSESSMENT PROCESS

This publication is designed to guide the board and the chief executive through an effective dialogue. The assessment process has three broad goals:

1. To clarify for the board and the chief executive their respective roles, responsibilities, and job expectations;

2. To provide insight into the board's perception of the executive's strengths, limitations, and overall performance; and

3. To foster the growth and development of the chief executive and the organization.

AN OPPORTUNITY FOR LEARNING

The assessment should be a learning exercise. It is not meant to be a report card, to assign blame, or to be used strictly as a basis for setting compensation. This assessment instrument provides tools to lead the board and the executive through a thoughtful discussion about the chief executive's past performance and future aspirations. It is only through discussion of this type that nonprofit leaders can chart courses of action and make progress in fulfilling their organizations' missions.

BoardSource offers consulting services to assist in chief executive assessment. For more information on these services, please call BoardSource at 202-452-6262, e-mail mail@boardsource.org, or write to Governance Consulting, BoardSource, Suite 900, 1828 L Street NW, Washington, DC 20036-5114.

The Questionnaire

This questionnaire is designed to help boards and chief executives assess the performance of the chief executive. It should take 30–45 minutes to complete. To encourage candor, the questionnaire does not ask for names. The confidential responses, along with the responses of fellow board members, will be summarized and shared with the chief executive at a meeting with a small committee of the board. Because the responses of the chief executive will be evaluated separately from those of the board, those results will not remain anonymous. Therefore, it is important for us to know whether you are the chief executive or a board member; please indicate your organizational role below.

Throughout the survey, each set of questions begins with a brief description of an important area of responsibility. Please read the descriptions and then answer the questions that follow. The questions measure how well board members believe the chief executive has met their expectations in carrying out various aspects of each responsibility. Answers can range on a scale from 1 to 3, with 1 representing "Failed To Meet Expectations" and 3 representing "Exceeded Expectations." There is also an option for answering "Not Applicable" if a particular question does not apply to the organization.

At the end of each section there is room for additional, open-ended comments. These responses will be especially helpful when the board and chief executive look for ways to strengthen both the executive's performance and that of the organization as a whole.

After the results have been tabulated, the board will meet in an executive session to discuss the key themes that are revealed. Then, the chief executive will meet with representatives of the board to review the results. During this meeting, the assessment results will be used to identify areas for personal growth and draft action plans will be developed for the chief executive's personal development. This meeting will also be a good opportunity to discuss ways in which the board can better support or complement the chief executive's work and to discuss mutual hopes for the future of the organization.

PLEASE INDICATE YOUR ROLE IN THE ORGANIZATION

I am: ☐ **The chief executive**   ☐ **A board member**

SECTION 1: ANNUAL PERFORMANCE GOALS

Annual performance goals help the chief executive set direction and priorities, and serve to clarify expectations between the board and the executive.

The chief executive's annual goals can focus on *organizational priorities* (e.g., increasing public awareness of the organization or doubling the membership), *leadership tasks* that the executive has been charged with (e.g., reorganizing a specific department in the organization or increasing the number of public appearances on behalf of the organization), or *professional development goals* (e.g., appropriately delegating responsibility to other staff or improving personal communication skills).

Please refer to the attached list of performance goals when responding to this section.
The following performance goals were established for the chief executive of your organization.

Please indicate whether the chief executive met your expectations in pursuing or achieving each of these goals:	Failed To Meet Expectations	Met Expectations	Exceeded Expectations	Not Applicable
1.1 Performance goal one	1 ☐	2 ☐	3 ☐	0 ☐
1.2 Performance goal two	1 ☐	2 ☐	3 ☐	0 ☐
1.3 Performance goal three	1 ☐	2 ☐	3 ☐	0 ☐
1.4 Performance goal four	1 ☐	2 ☐	3 ☐	0 ☐
1.5 Performance goal five	1 ☐	2 ☐	3 ☐	0 ☐
1.6 Performance goal six	1 ☐	2 ☐	3 ☐	0 ☐
1.7 Performance goal seven	1 ☐	2 ☐	3 ☐	0 ☐
1.8 Performance goal eight	1 ☐	2 ☐	3 ☐	0 ☐
1.9 Performance goal nine	1 ☐	2 ☐	3 ☐	0 ☐
1.10 Performance goal ten	1 ☐	2 ☐	3 ☐	0 ☐

Do you have specific comments about the chief executive's performance on these annual goals?

SECTION 2: CORE COMPETENCIES FOR NONPROFIT CHIEF EXECUTIVES

While there is no single model for effective nonprofit leaders, a number of core areas of responsibility are essential for success. These competencies — planning, administration, board relations, financial management, communications and public relations, and fundraising — will be covered in this section. There will also be an opportunity to include additional comments.

2.1 PLANNING

Planning for the future is one of the most critical leadership responsibilities of the chief executive. Working with the board, the chief executive must develop a shared vision for the future of the organization, build understanding around the mission, and develop appropriate goals and strategies to advance that mission.

Please indicate whether the chief executive met your expectations in the following areas:	Failed To Meet Expectations	Met Expectations	Exceeded Expectations	Not Applicable
2.1a In collaboration with the board, articulated a clear vision for the future of the organization	1 ☐	2 ☐	3 ☐	0 ☐
2.1b Used the mission of the organization as a guide in making decisions	1 ☐	2 ☐	3 ☐	0 ☐
2.1c Engaged the board in meaningful strategic thinking about the organization	1 ☐	2 ☐	3 ☐	0 ☐
2.1d Developed appropriate goals and objectives to advance the mission	1 ☐	2 ☐	3 ☐	0 ☐
2.1e Effectively led the staff in implementing strategic objectives and annual goals	1 ☐	2 ☐	3 ☐	0 ☐

Photocopying the BoardSource Assessment of the Chief Executive *tool is in violation of the BoardSource copyright.*

2.2 ADMINISTRATION

The chief executive has overall responsibility for the day-to-day operations of the organization. The chief executive works with staff to develop, maintain, and use the systems and resources that facilitate the effective operation of the organization.

Please indicate whether the chief executive met your expectations in the following areas:	Failed To Meet Expectations	Met Expectations	Exceeded Expectations	Not Applicable
2.2 a Displayed a thorough knowledge of the organization's mission area and programs	1 ☐	2 ☐	3 ☐	0 ☐
2.2 b Managed the organization efficiently on a day-to-day basis	1 ☐	2 ☐	3 ☐	0 ☐
2.2 c Managed the successful delivery of programs	1 ☐	2 ☐	3 ☐	0 ☐
2.2 d Recruited, developed, and retained the staff needed to implement the annual work plan	1 ☐	2 ☐	3 ☐	0 ☐
2.2 e Minimized risk by ensuring that appropriate and up-to-date organizational policies and procedures are in place	1 ☐	2 ☐	3 ☐	0 ☐
2.2 f Ensured compliance with all legal and regulatory requirements	1 ☐	2 ☐	3 ☐	0 ☐

2.3 BOARD RELATIONS

Together, the chief executive and the board form the leadership team of the organization. Each arm of the team draws upon its own unique strengths and abilities. The chief executive and board have joint responsibility for developing and maintaining a strong working relationship and a system for sharing information that enables the board to effectively carry out its governance role.

Please indicate whether the chief executive met your expectations in the following areas:	Failed to Meet Expectations	Met Expectations	Exceeded Expectations	Not Applicable
2.3a Maintained an effective working relationship with the board, characterized by open communication, respect, and trust	1 ☐	2 ☐	3 ☐	0 ☐
2.3b Working with the board chair, focused board meetings on topics of highest priority that needed board attention and involvement	1 ☐	2 ☐	3 ☐	0 ☐
2.3c Provided board members with the appropriate information needed to support informed decision making and effective governance	1 ☐	2 ☐	3 ☐	0 ☐
2.3d Engaged board members, collectively and individually, in understanding and making sense of the organization's environment, challenges, and potential	1 ☐	2 ☐	3 ☐	0 ☐

2.4 Financial Management

Ensuring that resources are managed wisely is especially important for a nonprofit organization operating in the public trust. The chief executive's role is to see that the organization's goals and strategic plan serve as the basis for sound financial management, that solid budgeting and accounting systems are in place, and that appropriate financial controls and risk management strategies protect the organization's assets.

Please indicate whether the chief executive met your expectations in the following areas:	Failed To Meet Expectations	Met Expectations	Exceeded Expectations	Not Applicable
2.4 a Made sound financial decisions and recommendations based on a thorough understanding of the organization's overall financial picture	1 ☐	2 ☐	3 ☐	0 ☐
2.4 b Allocated financial and human resources appropriately to achieve the organization's goals and objectives	1 ☐	2 ☐	3 ☐	0 ☐
2.4 c Presented the annual budget and financial statements in a timely and accurate manner for review and action by the board	1 ☐	2 ☐	3 ☐	0 ☐
2.4 d Implemented appropriate internal controls to protect the organization from fraud and abuse	1 ☐	2 ☐	3 ☐	0 ☐

2.5 COMMUNICATIONS AND PUBLIC RELATIONS

The chief executive serves as a primary spokesperson and "public face" for the organization. This role has three major components: effectively promoting the organization, advocating for the mission and work of the organization, and building relationships with the constituent or stakeholder groups critical to the success of the organization.

Please indicate whether the chief executive met your expectations in the following areas:	Failed To Meet Expectations	Met Expectations	Exceeded Expectations	Not Applicable
2.5 a Served as an articulate and effective spokesperson for the organization	1 ☐	2 ☐	3 ☐	0 ☐
2.5 b Served as a strong public advocate for the organization's mission and message	1 ☐	2 ☐	3 ☐	0 ☐
2.5 c Established and maintained positive relationships with individuals and groups that impact the success of the organization	1 ☐	2 ☐	3 ☐	0 ☐

2.6 FUNDRAISING

The chief executive, in partnership with the board and appropriate staff, is responsible for developing and implementing fundraising systems and strategies that enable the organization to meet its financial development goals and carry out its programs and operations.

Please indicate whether the chief executive met your expectations in the following areas:	Failed To Meet Expectations	Met Expectations	Exceeded Expectations	Not Applicable
2.6a Served as an effective fundraiser	1 ☐	2 ☐	3 ☐	0 ☐
2.6b Ensured that the organization developed appropriate fundraising strategies and policies	1 ☐	2 ☐	3 ☐	0 ☐
2.6c Motivated prospective donors by making a compelling case about the importance of the organization's work	1 ☐	2 ☐	3 ☐	0 ☐
2.6d Effectively involved the board in implementing the organization's fundraising program	1 ☐	2 ☐	3 ☐	0 ☐

Do you have specific comments about any of the chief executive's core competencies?

SECTION 3: PERSONAL LEADERSHIP QUALITIES

Beyond the core functional responsibilities of the chief executive, there are a number of additional leadership and interpersonal skills that are important to the chief executive's success.

3.1 LEADERSHIP SKILLS

Please indicate whether the chief executive met your expectations in demonstrating the following:	Failed To Meet Expectations	Met Expectations	Exceeded Expectations	Not Applicable
3.1a A clear commitment to the organization's mission and values	1 ☐	2 ☐	3 ☐	0 ☐
3.1b An ability to motivate and engage others in advancing the mission of the organization	1 ☐	2 ☐	3 ☐	0 ☐
3.1c An ability to learn from the successes and failures of the past in planning for the future	1 ☐	2 ☐	3 ☐	0 ☐
3.1d A willingness to ask difficult questions and challenge organizational assumptions	1 ☐	2 ☐	3 ☐	0 ☐
3.1e An awareness of trends and information in the external environment that may impact the organization	1 ☐	2 ☐	3 ☐	0 ☐
3.1f A sense of innovation and creativity	1 ☐	2 ☐	3 ☐	0 ☐

3.2 INTERPERSONAL SKILLS

Please indicate whether the chief executive met your expectations in demonstrating the following:	Failed To Meet Expectations	Met Expectations	Exceeded Expectations	Not Applicable
3.2 a Effective problem-solving skills	1 ☐	2 ☐	3 ☐	0 ☐
3.2 b Good judgment in decision making	1 ☐	2 ☐	3 ☐	0 ☐
3.2 c Effective communication skills	1 ☐	2 ☐	3 ☐	0 ☐
3.2 d The ability to build trusting relationships	1 ☐	2 ☐	3 ☐	0 ☐
3.2 e The ability to balance diverging and competing points of view	1 ☐	2 ☐	3 ☐	0 ☐
3.2 f The ability to accept constructive criticism	1 ☐	2 ☐	3 ☐	0 ☐

Do you have specific comments about the chief executive's personal leadership qualities?

SECTION 4: ACCOMPLISHMENTS AND CHALLENGES

While the quantitative ratings in the previous sections provide an important snapshot of the board's assessment of the chief executive in key areas of responsibility and performance, this section of the survey provides an opportunity to include thoughts and insights about the chief executive that cannot be captured in numeric scores. Please answer the following open-ended questions.

ASSESSING THE PAST

The following questions consider the overall achievements of the chief executive over the past year and will serve as the foundation for discussion between the board and chief executive.

4.1 What were the most significant achievements of the chief executive over the past year?

4.2 In the past year, what difficult issues did the organization face, and how did the chief executive address them?

4.3 Have any legal, ethical, or governance issues arisen with regard to the operations of the organization? How were these addressed?

PLANNING FOR THE FUTURE

While the majority of the questions in this assessment focus on past performance, the final questions look to the future. These questions will assist the board and chief executive in establishing the executive's performance goals and priorities for the upcoming year.

In thinking about the year ahead . . .

4.4 What are the two most important organizational priorities for the chief executive?

4.5 What are the two most important leadership tasks for the chief executive?

4.6 What are the two most important professional development goals for the chief executive?

About the Authors

Joshua Mintz is a partner at Cavanaugh, Hagan & Pierson. His work includes conducting organizational and leadership assessments to help organizations understand where they currently are, and facilitating strategic planning processes to help organizations identify where they would like to be in the future.

Along the way, Josh supports his clients' efforts by strengthening management and governance systems and structures, facilitating staff and leadership retreats, and by serving as a sounding board for clients as they think about the challenges and opportunities they face as they carry out their mission and goals. His practice focuses heavily on the needs of nonprofit and philanthropic organizations.

Josh received his Bachelor of Arts degree in Government from Georgetown University and his Master's of Science in Applied Behavioral Science from The Johns Hopkins University. He serves on the board of directors of College Bound and on the selection committee for the Washington Post Award for Excellence in Nonprofit Management. Josh lives in Washington, D.C., with his wife, Nicole, and their two sons.

Jane Pierson is a partner at Cavanaugh, Hagan & Pierson. Her practice focuses on the strategic, social, and political currents in organizations and how they shape the direction and culture of institutions and their governance structures. Her services include organization diagnosis and assessment; consulting to leadership and management teams; retreat and meeting facilitation; strategy development and strategic planning; governance and board/staff role clarification; chief executive and senior manager and board assessments; conflict management; consultation on reorganization; and organization change.

Ms. Pierson was a founder and former executive director of the National Women's Political Caucus and former Director of Legislative and Political Affairs at the American Federation of Government Employees of the AFL-CIO. She holds a Master of Science degree in Organization and Human Resource Development from the joint program of the American University and the NTL Institute. An experienced speaker and educator, Ms. Pierson was a Fellow at Harvard University's Institute of Politics at the Kennedy School of Government, and is a Fellow of the NTL Institute.